D1068693

Explorers & Exploration

The Travels of John and Sebastian Cabot

By Joanne Mattern
Illustrated by Patrick O'Brien

STECK-VAUGHN
ELEMENTARY · SECONDARY · ADULT · LIBRARY

A Harcourt Company

www.steck-vaughn.com

Produced by By George Productions, Inc.

Printed and bound in the United States of America
10 9 8 7 6 5 4 3 2 1 W 04 03 02 01 00

Illustration Acknowledgments
Pp 4, 6-7, 9, 14, 16-17, 24-25, 38, North Wind Picture Archives; pp 5, 12,
22, 26-27, 30-31, The New York Public Library; pp 34-35, 42, The
Mariners, Museum, Newport News, VA.
All other artwork is by Patrick O'Brien.

Contents

The Lure of the East

Most people know that the explorer Christopher Columbus was born in Genoa, Italy. Genoa was also the birthplace of another famous explorer. This explorer's name was Giovanni Caboto. He is better known by his English name, John Cabot. Along with his son Sebastian, John Cabot played an important role in the exploration of North America.

The city of Genoa, Italy

Statue of John and Sebastian Cabot

5

Giovanni Caboto was born sometime around 1450. Not much is known about his early life. Experts do know that his father was a merchant. Since Genoa was an important seaport, they also know that Giovanni was surrounded by boats and sailors throughout his childhood. It is not surprising that he loved the sea.

Another important seaport in Italy was the city of Venice. Today, Venice is part of Italy. But in Giovanni's time, it was independent. The city is built on a series of small islands. Instead of streets, there are canals filled with water.

Venice, Italy

Trade with other countries made Venice one of the richest places in Europe. Goods from all over the world were brought to Venice. From there the goods were sent on to other countries. The city was filled with ships that came from the Far East carrying spices, jewels, and silks. The Far East usually meant the countries of eastern Asia, including China, Japan, Korea, and Mongolia. Other ships came from northern Europe. They were filled with furs, silver, and steel.

Venice had over 3,000 galleys, or large ships. Venice had the greatest fleet of ships in Europe. When Giovanni was about ten years old, his father moved the family to Venice. Again, Giovanni was surrounded by sailors describing faraway lands and treasures.

When Giovanni Caboto grew up, he became a merchant, like his father. He became involved in the spice trade between Europe and the Far East. In the 1400s, spices were more valuable than jewels. In those days, the only way to keep meat from spoiling was to dry it or salt it. Dried and salted meat is tough and has little flavor. Spices were added in order to make the meat good to eat.

As a merchant, Giovanni did quite a bit of traveling. One of his most exciting trips took him to Mecca, a city in present-day Saudi Arabia. In those days, Europeans were not allowed to enter Mecca.

The temple at Mecca

This was because they were not Muslims. If they were caught, they were killed. However, Mecca was also an important trading city. Goods from countries in the Far East came through Mecca on their way to Europe. Giovanni wanted to see this busy place. He walked through the markets and streets, and talked to the merchants. But he was careful to keep his face covered so no one could see he was European.

While Giovanni was there, he learned a great deal about the spice trade. Now he wanted to know if there was a way to sail directly to the Far East without having to go through Venice.

By the 1480s, Giovanni had become an experienced seaman and navigator, someone who steers a ship. He was also known as a mapmaker. He had married and had three sons. One of them, Sebastian, was born in the late 1470s. Later, Sebastian would follow in his explorer father's footsteps.

Giovanni Caboto still wanted to travel to the Far East. He went to the rulers of Portugal and Spain and asked them to pay for a trip to look for a direct sea route to Asia across the northern part of the earth. Because the north is far away from the equator, it would make the trip shorter. Both countries turned him down. Spain had already hired Christopher Columbus to find a southern route to Asia. Portugal was more interested in reaching the Far East by traveling around the tip of Africa.

Sometime in the early 1490s, Giovanni moved his family to England. They settled in Bristol, another busy seaport. Giovanni Caboto changed his name to John Cabot. He continued to work as a merchant. He also continued to dream of an ocean voyage to the Far East.

Cabot knew that the English were interested in exploring new lands. He went to England's King Henry VII and told him of his idea about reaching

Asia by sailing across the northern Atlantic. King Henry liked Cabot's plan. On March 5, 1496, the king promised John Cabot five ships for his voyage.

King Henry did not entirely keep his promise. He gave Cabot only one ship and a crew of 18 men for his voyage. This ship was named the *Mathew*. It was a small vessel called a cog. It had three masts for sails and was only about 60 or 70 feet (18 or 21 m) long.

An English cog

∿

A New Found Land

The expedition left Bristol on May 20, 1497. One of the members of the crew was Cabot's teenage son Sebastian. It took the *Mathew* five weeks to cross the Atlantic Ocean.

At five o'clock on the morning of June 24, one of the sailors spotted land. Because it was the feast day of St. John the Baptist, Cabot named the place St. John. At first Cabot thought he was in China. In fact, he had landed in what is now eastern Canada. Experts are not sure exactly where Cabot landed. Some say Labrador. Others believe it was probably near present-day Cape Breton Island in Nova Scotia. This landing gave England a claim to land in North America.

As Cabot sailed along the shore, he realized that he was not in China. St. John was a large island. It took the *Mathew* a month to sail to the southern tip of St. John and back.

John Cabot and his son Sebastian leave on John Cabot's first voyage.

A painting that shows John Cabot landing on the shores of Labrador. Experts are not sure if he actually landed there.

Cabot and a few of his men went ashore to explore. They found a wilderness of thick forest. They also saw places where trees had been cut down and campfires had burned. They found animal traps and a pointed stick with holes drilled at both ends. Later, Cabot saw people moving through the trees. But he never met the people who lived on the island. Since he did not have many men with him, he decided to return to his ship.

The waters around St. John were so full of fish that one had only to lower a basket into the water to catch several.

John Cabot was considered a successful explorer.

At the southern tip of the island, Cabot saw deep, open water to the west. He believed that China was not far away. However, Cabot did not have enough men to explore any farther, so he returned to England.

Cabot and his crew landed in Bristol on August 6, 1497, after an easy two-week voyage. From there, Cabot went to London to talk to the king. King Henry was thrilled to hear of Cabot's success. He gave Cabot a large sum of money and promised to pay for a larger trip to explore this "new found land," as the king called it.

Word of Cabot's discovery spread quickly. He soon became a popular hero in England. People called him the "Great Admiral." Crowds of people followed him everywhere. Cabot was filled with pride at his new importance. He walked around London wearing fine clothes. Cabot did not forget the men who traveled with him. He gave the members of his crew rewards of titles and lands.

On John Cabot's second voyage,
the ships sailed through many storms.

John Cabot's Last Voyage

In early May 1498, John Cabot was ready to sail across the Atlantic Ocean from England. This time, King Henry was more generous. He gave the explorer five ships. Cabot carried an official paper from King Henry giving him permission to start a colony in the new land. He also planned to set up a trading center to ship spices back to England.

This trip did not go well. Soon after the fleet left England, one of the ships was damaged. It had to sail to Ireland for repairs. Cabot and the other ships sailed on into the Atlantic Ocean. However, something terrible must have happened, because Cabot and his crew were never heard from again.

What happened to John Cabot? Experts think that he and his ships probably went down at sea during a storm. But they do not know whether Cabot made it to North America before he was lost. Some experts believe that Cabot returned to Newfoundland and then sailed down to the Chesapeake Bay, in what is now Virginia. Others think that at least one of his ships sailed as far as the Caribbean Sea.

Why do they think this? In 1499, a Spanish explorer named Alonzo de Hojeda sailed to South America. Along the way, he came upon some English ships near the Bahamas. These are a group of islands in the Atlantic Ocean southeast of Florida and north of Cuba. The only Englishmen who could have been exploring the area at that time were Cabot and his men. Some experts believe that Hojeda might have met Cabot himself.

Other experts think that Cabot was lost on the journey back to England, but that some of his crew survived and returned to Bristol. However, no one has found any written accounts or other proof that anyone from Cabot's second voyage returned to England. And Cabot himself was never seen again.

Another Cabot Sets Sail

By the early 1500s, Europeans realized that the lands Christopher Columbus and John Cabot had reached were not part of Asia. They were part of a different continent, North America. But this did not make the Europeans less eager to explore these new places. Perhaps these places were as rich as Asia! Or perhaps there was a Northwest Passage, a way around or through this other continent, so European ships could reach Asia after all. Many explorers searched for this passage for many years before they realized it did not exist.

Sebastian Cabot had traveled to the "new found land" (or possibly Labrador) on his father's first voyage in 1497. By 1508, Sebastian was a grown man. He was a skilled mapmaker and navigator, just as his father had been. Sebastian wanted to follow in his father's footsteps in another way. He wanted to be a famous explorer.

Sebastian Cabot was on his father's 1497 voyage, which may have reached Labrador.

In 1508, Sebastian Cabot went to King Henry VII, who had given money for his father's voyages. Sebastian asked the king to allow him to explore North America in search of the Northwest Passage. King Henry agreed.

In spring 1508, Sebastian Cabot left Bristol with two ships. The ships sailed northward to Greenland. They were so far north the sailors saw icebergs floating in the ocean. Then Sebastian turned west until he reached the coast of Canada. The ships sailed into a waterway leading inland to a large body of water.

Cabot was delighted. He was sure this waterway led to China. Historians think that he was actually in what is now called Hudson Bay.

The crew did not share Sebastian's excitement. The sailors were cold and uncomfortable. They wanted to go home. They threatened to mutiny, or take over the ship, if he did not turn back.

25

Sebastian had no choice but to sail back to the Atlantic Ocean. Sebastian's ships sailed down the coast, looking for a warmer climate. They traveled as far south as Cape Hatteras in what is now North Carolina. Sebastian hoped to find another passage leading to the Far East. There was none. Disappointed, he finally turned the ships around and sailed home to England.

When Sebastian and his men arrived in Bristol in 1509, they received some bad news. King Henry VII had died. Now his son, Henry VIII, was on the throne. The new king had no interest in exploring new lands. He would not pay for another trip to North America.

Sebastian Cabot did not tell anyone that he might have found the Northwest Passage. He wanted to make another voyage and explore it himself.

Sebastian Cabot

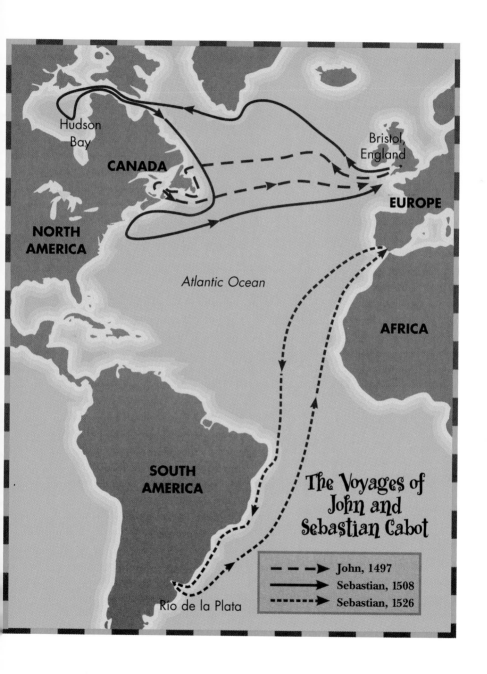

Hudson
Bay

CANADA

Bristol,
England

EUROPE

NORTH
AMERICA

Atlantic Ocean

AFRICA

SOUTH
AMERICA

The Voyages of
John and
Sebastian Cabot

Rio de la Plata

- - - → John, 1497
——— → Sebastian, 1508
····· → Sebastian, 1526

A Dream Comes True

In 1512, Sebastian Cabot traveled to Spain with an English army to help Spain fight a war against the French. He missed the sea, though, so he offered to be a mapmaker for Spain. Since Spain and England were allies, or friends, at that time, King Henry let Sebastian stay in Spain.

Cabot spent the next five years making maps for the Spanish navy. He also taught others how to navigate and sail. Later, Sebastian married a Spanish woman.

Around the year 1516, Sebastian was given an important new position. He became a naval aide to the Spanish king, Ferdinand V. Sebastian used his new job to try to return to sea. He talked to King Ferdinand about returning to North America. The king was interested, but before he could do anything he died in 1516. Once again, Sebastian had to wait.

In 1517, Sebastian went back to England for a visit. While he was there, he tried to get ships and men for a voyage to North America to explore what he thought was the Northwest Passage. But he was unable to get the support he needed. Disappointed, Sebastian went back to Spain.

Spain's new king was Charles I. He liked Sebastian very much. He made Cabot pilot major, or chief navigator, of Spain. It was Sebastian's job to keep all the maps and charts up to date.

Although Sebastian had an important job, what he really wanted to do was to explore what he thought was the Northwest Passage. In 1520, he began to talk with the English government about a voyage. Sebastian had to keep these talks secret, though. He would have been in a lot of trouble if Spain found out about them. The Spanish government had just sent Ferdinand Magellan on a trip around the world to Asia. It did not want anyone—and certainly not its pilot major—making the same voyage for another country!

Sebastian Cabot wanted to explore the Northwest Passage.

**One of Sebastian Cabot's ships ran
aground in the Río de la Plata.**

Sebastian could not get any support for his voyage from England. Then he got more bad news. Somehow, an official in the government of Venice had learned of Sebastian's meetings with England and of his claim to have found the Northwest Passage. The official threatened to tell the Spanish government what he had done unless Sebastian told the government of Venice where the passage was located.

Sebastian agreed, but he did not keep his side of the bargain! He knew that his only chance of returning to North America was to keep the location of the Northwest Passage a secret.

Finally, in 1526, Spain gave Sebastian four ships and told him to sail to South America. Cabot was to follow Magellan's route around South America and across the Pacific Ocean to the Spice Islands in the East Indies.

Sebastian went as far as present-day Argentina. There, he met some Spaniards. They told him there were huge amounts of gold and silver farther inland. Cabot did not obey the orders he was given, to sail around South America to the Pacific Ocean. Instead, he and his crew sailed up a river in Argentina now called the Río de la Plata.

It was a bad trip from the start. One of the ships sank.

The sailors fought with the native people they met along the way. In one battle, 20 of Sebastian's men were killed. Finally, the crew mutinied. Sebastian killed some of the crew members who had turned against him. He put others ashore in the jungle with only a few weapons and little food, and left them there.

Sebastian sent some of his crew back to Spain to bring back more men and supplies. In order to get support, he lied. He sent a message to the Spanish government saying he had discovered a land rich in gold and silver. However, no men or supplies ever arrived.

Finally, after four years, Sebastian Cabot gave up. He and his remaining men returned to Spain.

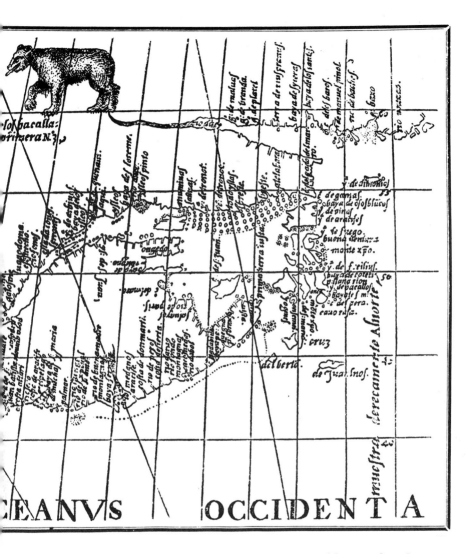

A section of Sebastian Cabot's 1544 world map showing
North America.

Things did not go well for Sebastian Cabot back in Spain, either. The members of his crew were angry at the way he'd led the trip. They brought him to court and said that he had treated his crew badly. They also said that he had not obeyed his orders for the voyage. Sebastian was found guilty. He was sent away and ordered not to return. As a result, he would have to live in Africa for three years.

The Spanish king Charles I was still Sebastian's friend. When the king heard about Cabot's punishment, he said that the explorer did not have to go to Africa. Sebastian went back to being Spain's pilot major.

Sebastian drew a new map of the world. It was published in 1544. This map included the places John Cabot had reached in North America. It also included the places Sebastian had reached during his own travels in South America. The lands that were reached recently by Spanish and Portuguese explorers were on the new map as well.

Sebastian's map soon became very important. It contained so much new information that later maps of the world were based on it.

The Company of Merchant Adventurers

Although Sebastian Cabot had lived and worked in Spain for more than 30 years, in 1547 King Edward VI of England offered him an important job. Sebastian's new job was to arrange trade agreements between England and other European countries.

This job was interesting and paid very well. Sebastian was good at his work. However, he had not forgotten his dream of finding a shortcut to Asia. Neither had the English merchants. In the early 1550s, some English merchants formed a group that was called the Company of Merchant Adventurers. Sebastian was named the head of the company. The merchants wanted to look for a Northeast Passage. This was a sea route that connected the Atlantic and Pacific oceans along the northern coasts of Europe and Asia.

By now Sebastian was too old to take part in the voyage. But that did not stop him from taking part in the project. Sebastian worked as the chief planner. He had the company buy three ships for the journey. Two skilled seamen, Sir Hugh Willoughby and Richard Chancellor, were picked as captain and chief navigator. The ships left England on May 20, 1553.

After sailing along the coast of Norway, the ships became separated in a bad storm. Willoughby's ship and one of the other ships landed on the Kola Peninsula, in Lapland. Willoughby and his men froze to death there during the winter. Chancellor's ship sailed to a land called Muscovy, the country that today is known as Russia.

Before returning to England in 1554, Chancellor met the czar, or ruler, of Muscovy. Chancellor was able to arrange a trade agreement with the Russian leader. Although a Northeast Passage to China had not been found, the trade agreement was very profitable. The Company of Merchant Adventurers changed its name to the Muscovy Company. Its members grew rich trading English cloth for Russian furs and lumber.

Sir Hugh Willoughby froze to death during his 1553 expedition to find the Northeast Passage around Norway.

Sebastian Cabot died in England in 1557. His dream of finding the Northwest and Northeast passages never came true. Yet he is an important person in the history of European exploration. Together with his father, John, Sebastian helped pave the way for the English to settle North America. Without their work, today's world might be a very different place.

John and Sebastian Cabot are both important people in the history of European exploration.

The cross-staff was a tool used by
navigators in the 1400s and 1500s.

Other Events of the 16th Century
(1501 – 1600)

During the century that Sebastian Cabot was sailing, events were happening in other parts of the world. Some of these were:

1502   Portuguese navigator Vasco da Gama makes his second voyage to India in order to expand trade.

1521   Hernán Cortés, a Spanish conquistador, conquers the Aztec Empire in Mexico.

1524   Giovanni da Verrazano, an Italian sailor, explores the coast of North America from North Carolina to Maine.

1534   Francisco Pizarro of Spain conquers the Inca Empire in Peru.

1571   Portuguese create colony in Angola, Africa.

1578   Moroccans destroy Portuguese power in northwest Africa.

Time Line

1450?	Giovanni Caboto is born in Genoa, Italy.
1461?	Giovanni moves to Venice with his family.
Late 1470s	Giovanni's son Sebastian is born.
Early 1490s	Giovanni moves to Bristol, England, and changes his name to John Cabot.
March 1496	King Henry VII of England allows John Cabot to try to find a route to the Far East by sailing west across the Atlantic Ocean.
May 20, 1497	John Cabot leaves England on the ship *Mathew*.
June 24, 1497	The *Mathew* lands on an island in eastern Canada. Cabot names it St. John.
August 6, 1497	After exploring the island, John Cabot returns to England.
May 1498	John Cabot begins another western voyage. He is never heard from again.
1508	Sebastian Cabot sails to Greenland and into what is now Hudson Bay in Canada. He thinks he has discovered the Northwest Passage. Cold weather and an angry crew force him to return to England.
1512	Sebastian Cabot moves to Spain and becomes a mapmaker for the Spanish navy.

1517 and 1520	Sebastian Cabot cannot get English support for a northwest voyage.
1526	The Spanish government sends Sebastian Cabot to follow Ferdinand Magellan's route around South America to the Far East. Cabot explores the Río de la Plata in Argentina instead.
1530	Sebastian Cabot returns to Spain and is tried in court for disobeying orders. He is found guilty but King Charles I does not want him punished.
1544	Sebastian Cabot publishes a new map of the world. It includes places reached by his father, himself, and other explorers.
1547	Cabot returns to England to take charge of England's naval affairs.
Early 1550s	Sebastian Cabot is named the leader of a new company called the Company of Merchant Adventurers. He is the chief planner for a voyage to find a Northeast Passage to China around the coast of Norway.
1554	Richard Chancellor, navigator of the voyage, returns from Muscovy with a good trade agreement.
1557	Sebastian Cabot dies in England.

Glossary

admiral (AD-muh-ruhl) An officer in the navy

aide (AYD) A person who works with others to help them do their job

allies (AL-ize) People or nations that support one another

canals (kuh-NALZ) Waterways dug across land

cog (KAHG) A small sailing vessel

colony (KOL-uh-nee) An area that has been settled by people from another country and is governed by that country

continent (KON-tuh-nent) One of Earth's seven great landmasses (North America, South America, Africa, Asia, Europe, Australia, Antarctica)

East Indies (IN-deez) A name that once referred mainly to India but that now includes Indonesia and Southeast Asia

expedition (ek-spuh-DISH-uhn) A long journey for a special purpose

Far East The countries of East Asia, including China, Japan, Korea, and Mongolia; sometimes the countries of Southeast Asia and the islands of Malaysia are included.

galley (GAL-ee) a long boat with oars

Lapland (LAP-land) The region of northern Europe that is above the Arctic Circle

merchant (MUR-chuhnt) Someone who sells goods for profit

Muscovy (MUS-koh-vee) The former name of Russia

mutiny (MYOOT-uh-nee) A rebellion in which sailors refuse to obey the captain and take control of the ship

naval (NAY-vuhl) Having to do with a navy

navigation (na-vuh-GAY-shun) Using maps and instruments to find the way

navigator (NA-vuh-gay-tur) A person who steers a ship

Northeast Passage (north-eest PAS-ij) A sea route connecting the Atlantic and Pacific oceans along the northern coasts of Europe and Asia

seaport (SEE-port) A city or town with a harbor where ships can dock

Spice Islands A group of islands in Indonesia now called the Moluccas that are rich in spices

Index